FRANCIS FRITH'S

A Taste of

CUMBRIA

& THE LAKE DISTRICT

REGIONAL RECIPES FROM CUMBRIA AND THE LAKES

Illustrated with historical photographs from
The Francis Frith Collection

FRANCIS FRITH'S

A Taste of
CUMBRIA
& THE LAKE DISTRICT

Ulverston, King Street 1912 64396

Compiled by Julia Skinner

First published in the United Kingdom by
The Francis Frith Collection exclusively for Dorrigo in 2009.
Paperback Edition ISBN 978-1-84589-438-2

British Library Cataloguing in Publication Data

A Taste of Cumbria and the Lake District
Julia Skinner

The Francis Frith Collection®
Frith's Barn, Teffont,
Salisbury, Wiltshire SP3 5QP
Tel: +44 (0) 1722 716 376
Email: info@francisfrith.co.uk
www.francisfrith.com

Printed and bound in Malta

Front Cover: Grange-over-Sands, The Pier 1914 67426t
The colour-tinting in this image is for illustrative purposes only, and is not intended
to be historically accurate.

Every attempt has been made to contact copyright holders of illustrative material.
We will be happy to give full acknowledgement in future editions for any items not
credited. Any information should be directed to The Francis Frith Collection.

As with any historical database, the Francis Frith archive is constantly being
corrected and improved, and the publishers would welcome information on
omissions or inaccuracies.

CONTENTS

INTRODUCTION

—·—

Travel around Cumbria and the Lake District through the pages of this book and discover a selection of the delicious traditional food of the area, as well as some of the stories and fascinating facts behind the recipes. Your journey will be given added savour by the historical images taken by photographers from The Francis Frith Collection, showing the people and places of this region in the past. 'Cumbria' is a modern county that has only been in existence since 1974, formed from the old county of Cumberland together with parts of Westmorland and Lancashire; the names of these old counties are reflected in the names of many of the recipes in this book. Cumbria also includes the Lake District National Park, an area of outstanding natural beauty.

Regional traditional dishes were developed from the local produce that was available to thrifty housewives who had to feed large, hungry families on a limited budget. Many of the old recipes also reflect the limited cookery techniques that were available in the past, as well as the skills of the cooks who were able to provide cheap and tasty meals with only a fire, a skillet and a cauldron to cook with, often producing the historical version of 'boil in the bag' meals.

This book is not intended to provide a comprehensive collection of the local recipes of the region, and some recipes are modern interpretations using some of the fine local produce that the area is famous for, but we hope that the food described within these pages, as well as the descriptions of traditional customs and local dialect words, will provide you with a taste of Cumbria and the Lakes.

Windermere 1886 18663

SOUPS

Bardsea, The Beach 1895 35914

RECIPE

— . —

Cockle Soup

Morecambe Bay stretches along the coast of Cumbria as well as Lancashire, and is Britain's second largest bay after the Wash. Cockles and brown shrimps have been farmed here for centuries, an important local industry.

1.2 litres/2 pints measure of cockles
25g/1oz butter
25g/1oz plain flour
300ml/ ½ pint milk
2 sticks of celery
Salt and pepper
Chopped fresh parsley

Scrub the cockles well, then boil them in salted water until they open – discard any cockles that do not open. Drain off the cooking liquid and reserve. Make a white roux with the butter and flour, then gradually mix in 600ml (1 pint) of the cockle water and the milk whilst bringing the mixture to the boil, stirring continually, until it has thickened and formed a smooth consistency. Add the finely chopped celery, reduce the heat and simmer for 30 minutes, then add the shelled cockles, most of the chopped parsley and salt and pepper to taste. Cook for a few minutes longer before serving, garnished with the reserved chopped parsley.

— . —

Barrow-in-Furness, Walney Bridge 1912 64407

RECIPE

⸺ · ⸺

Mutton Broth

Mutton is the meat of a fully grown sheep. It was once staple fare throughout the country, and is now starting to make a comeback. In the Lake District mutton comes from Herdwick sheep. If mutton is unavailable, use scrag end of lamb for this recipe, which makes a good hearty soup for cold winter days.

450g/1 lb scrag end of mutton, or lamb, cut into small pieces
2 carrots
1 medium turnip
1 onion
25g/1oz pearl barley
Salt and pepper
A sprig of fresh parsley
1.75 litres/3 pints of water

Place the meat in a large saucepan with the water. Peel the turnip and onion, and chop the carrot, turnip and onion into small pieces. Put the chopped vegetables and the pearl barley into the saucepan with the meat, and season to taste with salt and pepper. Bring to the boil, then reduce the heat, cover the pan and leave to simmer gently for 2 hours.

Just before serving, remove any bones from the broth. Finely chop the parsley and add to the broth, then serve piping hot, with hunks of brown bread.

⸺ · ⸺

Morland, General View c1955 M98008

FISH AND SHELLFISH

Grange-over-Sands, The Beach 1912 64347

RECITE

— · —

Potted Shrimps

Morecambe Bay is famous for particularly delicious brown shrimps, and potted shrimps are a favourite local delicacy.

> 225g/8oz unsalted butter
> 1 tablespoonful water
> 1 teaspoonful ground mace
> 2 good pinches cayenne pepper
> Freshly grated nutmeg, a generous helping
> 450g/1 lb fresh shrimps (or 350g/ ¾ lb frozen shrimps
>   or prawns, defrosted)
> Salt

First of all, make clarified butter: melt the butter slowly in a small pan with the water, taking care not to let it brown. Pour the melted butter into a bowl to cool, and place in the refrigerator and leave until the butter has hardened. Remove the solid butter (this is the clarified butter) and discard the liquid which has settled beneath it. Melt 115g/4oz of the clarified butter in a large saucepan with the spices, then add the shrimps or prawns, lower the heat right down and let them steep in the hot butter for 10 minutes – they must not cook in the heat or they will become tough. Taste for seasoning and add salt at this point, if needed. Pour the shrimps or prawns with the butter into small pots, and leave until the butter has set. Melt the remaining clarified butter and pour enough over the top of each pot to form a seal. Allow to cool, then keep in the refrigerator until needed. Take out of the refrigerator for about half an hour before serving, to allow the chill to go off, which gives the spiced butter more flavour. Serve with hot toast or crusty bread.

— · —

Cockermouth, Main Street 1906 54992

RECITE

—·—

Cumberland Stuffed Herrings with Mustard Sauce

The tradition of fishing is well-established along Cumbria's coast, and one local delicacy is stuffed herrings served with mustard sauce. The use of mustard with herrings is said to have been a culinary tradition introduced by the Vikings, who settled this area over a thousand years ago. The sharpness of the mustard cuts through the oiliness of the fish.

4 large herrings
3 heaped tablespoonfuls fresh white
   breadcrumbs
1 heaped teaspoonful finely chopped
   parsley
A squeeze of lemon juice
Grated rind of half a lemon
Salt and black pepper
Oil for frying
25g/1oz butter

Mustard Sauce
40g/1½ oz butter
25g/1oz plain flour
450ml/ ¾ pint milk
Salt and black pepper
1 level tablespoonful dry mustard
   powder
1 tablespoonful wine vinegar
1 level teaspoonful caster sugar
Lemon wedges and fresh parsley sprigs
   for garnish

Remove the heads from the herrings, clean, gut and bone them. Wash the herrings and pat them thoroughly dry. Put the breadcrumbs, parsley, lemon juice and lemon rind in a basin; season lightly with salt and freshly ground black pepper. Melt the butter and stir into the breadcrumbs to bind the mixture, which should now be moist, but crumbly. Stuff the herrings with the breadcrumb mixture, and if necessary secure them with wooden cocktail sticks. Slash the skins crossways two or three times on each side; brush the herrings with oil and wrap each in foil. Put the herrings in a well-buttered deep baking dish; cover with lightly buttered greaseproof paper and bake in the centre of a pre-heated oven at 200°C/400°F/Gas Mark 6 for 35-40 minutes. For the mustard sauce, melt 25g/1oz of the butter in a pan; stir in the flour and cook for 1 minute. Gradually stir in the milk, beating well until the sauce is quite smooth. Bring to the boil and simmer for 2-3 minutes; season with salt and pepper. Blend the mustard powder with the vinegar and stir into the sauce; add the sugar. Check seasoning and stir in the remaining butter. Transfer the baked herrings to a hot serving dish and garnish with wedges of lemon and sprigs of parsley. Serve the mustard sauce separately.

—·—

RECIPE

—·—

Fish Pudding

Large catches of sea trout, cod and whiting are brought into Cumbria's sea ports, especially to Whitehaven. In 1754 four large fishing vessels, or 'busses', from Whitehaven were attacked by crews of the herring fleet from the Isle of Man. The Manxmen resented the way that the Whitehaven men could flout the Manx fishing regulations that they themselves were bound by.

> 225g/8oz filleted cod or whiting
> 115g/4oz butter
> 115g/4oz fresh breadcrumbs
> 4 tablespoonfuls of milk
> 115g/4oz mushrooms
> 4 eggs
> Salt and pepper
> Anchovy sauce

Pre-heat the oven to 200°C/400°F/Gas Mark 6.

Melt the butter in a large, heavy-bottomed saucepan, and add the fish. Cover the pan with its lid and stew the fish gently until it is tender. Soak the breadcrumbs in the milk, and when the fish is cooked mash the fish and breadcrumbs together. Finely chop the mushrooms and add to the fish mixture. Beat the eggs and add to the mixture, season to taste with salt and pepper and combine the mixture well together.

Turn the fish mixture into a greased 450g/1 lb loaf tin, and bake in the pre-heated oven for 30 minutes. Turn out of the tin and serve hot, cut into slices, with anchovy sauce.

—·—

Grange-over-Sands, The Pier 1914 67426

Potted Char

A rare and unusual freshwater fish that is only found in the deep waters of the Lakes, especially around Windermere, is the char. This is a relative of the salmon, and is believed to be a very old species of fish that was left behind in the inland lakes at the end of the last Ice Age, as the glaciers melted. Char has a delicately-flavoured flesh with a pinkish tinge. It is caught with long fishing lines weighted with metal spinners, and is usually eaten served in a pie, or potted. Potted char was very popular as a breakfast dish in the 17th, 18th and 19th centuries, when it was served in special 'char dishes' made of white china decorated with pictures of the fish, which are collectors' items today.

Bowness-on-Windermere, The Ferry Boat 1896 38802

Thirlmere, From Hell How 1892 30562

RECIPE

—·—

Salmon with Cucumber Sauce

Freshwater fish, such as trout and salmon, inhabit the Lakes and many of the rivers that flow down to the sea through Cumbria from the Pennines and Cheviots. Salmon was once so plentiful in the area that in Kendal a school's rule book stipulated that the schoolboys should not be 'compelled to dine on salmon or fish in general more than 3 days a week.' In Victorian times a popular way of serving cold salmon was with a cucumber sauce. This recipe is an ideal dish for hot summer days.

> 1.8kg/4 lbs salmon, gutted and scaled
> A small amount of melted butter, for brushing on to the salmon
> 3 parsley or thyme sprigs
> Half a lemon, cut into 2 further segments
> 1 large cucumber, peeled
> 25g/1oz butter
> 115ml/4 fl oz dry white wine
> 3 tablespoonfuls of finely chopped dill
> 4 tablespoonfuls of sour cream, or natural yogurt if preferred
> Salt and pepper

Pre-heat the oven to 220°C/425°F/Gas Mark 7.

Season the salmon and brush it inside and out with melted butter. Place the herbs and lemon in the cavity. Wrap the salmon in foil, folding the edges together securely, then bake in the pre-heated oven for 15 minutes. Remove the fish from the oven and leave in the foil for 1 hour, then remove the skin from the salmon.

Meanwhile, halve the peeled cucumber lengthways, scoop out the seeds, and dice the flesh. Place the cucumber in a colander, sprinkle lightly with salt, leave for about 30 minutes to allow the superfluous liquid to drain, then rinse well and pat dry.

Heat the butter in a small saucepan, add the cucumber and cook for about 2 minutes, until translucent but not soft. Add the wine to the pan and boil briskly until the cucumber is dry. Stir the dill and sour cream or yogurt into the cucumber. Season to taste and serve immediately with the salmon.

—·—

Ambleside, Woman Crossing the Stepping Stones
1888 20484x

RECIPE

— . —

Baked Lake Trout

4 lake trout, gutted, cleaned and washed

4 sprigs of fresh parsley, finely chopped

4 sprigs of lemon thyme, finely chopped

75g/3oz butter, softened to room temperature

Salt and pepper

150ml/ ¼ pint white wine

Lemon wedges and parsley sprigs to garnish

Pre-heat the oven to 180°C/350°F/Gas Mark 4.

Mix the chopped herbs into 50g (2oz) of the butter. Divide the herb butter into four pieces, and put one piece into the cavity of each fish. Place the fish closely together in an ovenproof serving dish, laying them alternately head to tail to fit into the dish, and season to taste. Pour the wine over the fish. Cover with foil, and bake in the pre-heated oven for 20-25 minutes, until the fish is tender.

When the fish are cooked, remove the dish from the oven and dot the fish with the remaining herb butter, cut into small knobs, then replace the foil cover and bake for a further 10 minutes. Serve the fish garnished with lemon wedges and parsley sprigs.

— . —

MEAT, POULTRY AND GAME

STILL AT THE FRONT !

THE "ALBIONETTE"

Huge numbers of sheep are reared on the hill farms and moorlands of Cumbria, where hardy breeds such as the Swaledale can withstand the cold winds and bitter winters of the uplands. Many of the regional dishes use lamb, and Shepherd's Pie, a favourite dish all over England, is said to have originated in this part of the country.

'Sheep Meets' have been held in Cumbria for hundreds of years, when sheep that have wandered can be returned to their owners. Shepherding can be a solitary occupation and these occasions allow the shepherds to socialise together and enjoy traditional fare such as Tattie-Pot and Apple Pie.

RECIPE

—·—

Tattie-Pot

675g/1½ lbs potatoes
2 onions
225g/8oz carrots
1 small turnip
600ml/1 pint stock
450g/1 lb lean lamb, cut into cubes
1 black pudding, cut into slices
Salt and pepper

Oven temperature: 180°C/350°F/Gas Mark 4.

Put the cubed meat and sliced black pudding into a casserole dish. Cut the carrots, onions and turnip into slices, and add to the casserole. Pour the stock over, and season to taste with salt and pepper. Cut the potatoes into thick slices and arrange them in a layer on top of the vegetables in the casserole.

Cook in a moderate oven for 2-3 hours, until the potatoes are tender, and golden brown. The casserole lid can be removed for the last 30 minutes if liked, to crisp the potatoes.

Tattie-Pot is traditionally served with cold pickled red cabbage.

—·—

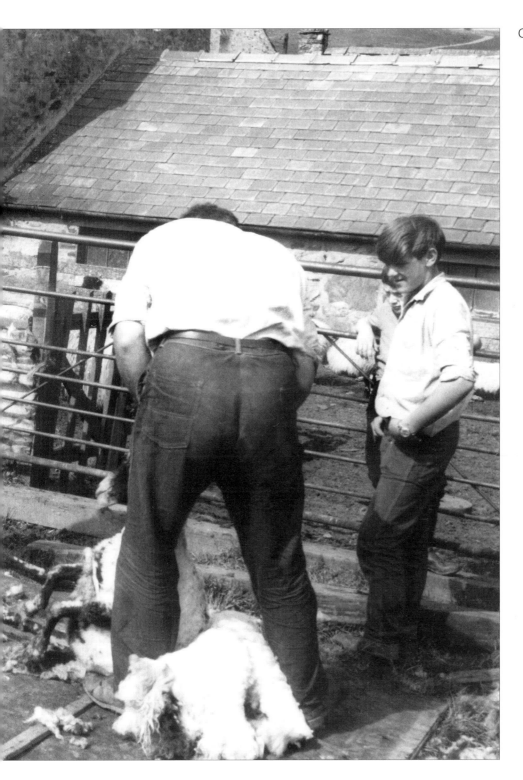

Caldbeck, Sheep
Shearing c1955
C567031

Greenodd, Main Street 1921 70700

RECIPE

—·—

Roast Lamb with Garlic and Rosemary

A leg or shoulder of lamb, allowing about 350g/12 oz
   meat on the bone per person
2-3 peeled cloves of garlic, sliced into small slivers
3-4 sprigs of fresh rosemary
Salt and pepper
25g/1oz butter, melted

Pre-heat the oven to 230°C/450°F/Gas Mark 8.

Using a sharp knife, cut a number of slits in the skin all over the meat, and rub the joint with salt and pepper. Insert alternate sprigs of rosemary and slivers of garlic into the slits in the meat. Dribble the melted butter over the joint, then stand it in a roasting tin.

Place the meat in the centre of the pre-heated hot oven, then immediately reduce the heat to 180°C/350°F/Gas Mark 4. Roast – without basting – for 25 minutes per 450g (1 lb) then a further 25 minutes (or just a further 15-20 minutes if you prefer your lamb pink).

—·—

Ambleside, The White Lion and Royal Oak Hotels 1912 64303

Hawkshead, The Square 1929 82372

RECITE

— . —

Westmorland Sweet Pie

In the past, mincemeat contained meat as well as dried fruit, hence the name. A sweet pie made with minced mutton or lamb, dried fruit and spices was the traditional fare at Christmas time in Cumberland and Westmorland.

For the pastry:
350g/12oz plain flour
75g/3oz butter or margarine
75g/3oz lard
A small amount of water, to mix
A small amount of milk, to glaze

For the pie:
225g/8oz lamb, minced or diced
675g/1½ lbs mixed dried fruit –
    currants, raisins, sultanas, mixed peel
115g/4oz soft brown sugar
4 tablespoonfuls of rum
A good pinch of ground mace
A good pinch of freshly grated nutmeg
A good pinch of ground cinnamon
Salt and freshly grated black pepper

First, make the pastry: rub the butter or margarine and lard into the flour until the mixture resembles fine breadcrumbs. Add just enough water to form a soft dough, and knead the dough lightly until it is smooth and pliable. Leave the dough to rest in a cool place for 30 minutes.

Pre-heat the oven to 200°C/400°F/Gas Mark 6.

Mix the minced or diced lamb with the mixed dried fruit. Add the rum, sugar, mace, nutmeg and cinnamon, season with salt and pepper and mix it all well together. Divide the pastry into two halves, roll out one half on a lightly floured surface and use it to line a greased large, shallow ovenproof pie dish. Put the filling into the pie dish. Roll out the remaining pastry and use it to make a lid for the pie dish, moistening the edges of the pastry and crimping firmly to seal them together. Prick the pastry lid all over with a fork to make small holes for steam to escape during cooking, then brush the pastry lid with a little milk to glaze. Bake in the pre-heated oven for about 30 minutes, until the pastry is crisp and golden.

— . —

Cumberland Sausage

Cumberland Sausage has a high meat content and is seasoned with spices and herbs such as sage and marjoram. It is made in a long coil, rather than individual sausages. It is sold by the length rather than by weight – sometimes being made in lengths up to1.2 metres (4 feet) long.

Penrith, Cornmarket c1955 P33013

RECIPE

Cumberland-style Baked Ham

1 ham, about 4.5 kg (10 lbs) in weight
Juice of half a lemon
50g/2oz dried breadcrumbs
25g/1oz soft brown sugar
1 teaspoonful made English mustard

Soak the ham overnight in cold water. Place the ham in a large saucepan with the lemon juice, and cover with fresh cold water. Bring to the boil, cover the pan and simmer gently for 3½ hours, replenishing the pan with more boiling water from time to time, and making sure that the pan does not boil dry. When cooked, remove the ham from the pan and reserve 150ml (¼ pint) of the cooking stock. (The cooking stock should not be discarded, as it can be kept to use as a base for soups, or it can be used to make Pease Pudding – see the recipe on page 40.)

Strip off the skin from the ham. With a sharp knife, mark a diamond pattern on the fat left beneath the skin. Mix the breadcrumbs with the sugar and mustard, and spread the mixture all over the ham. Place the ham in a roasting tin, and pour in 150ml (¼ pint) of the ham stock that the ham was boiled in. Cover with foil and bake in the pre-heated oven for about 30 minutes, to finish.

The ham can then be eaten hot or cold, and is delicious served with Cumberland Sauce – see recipe on page 37.

Wild game

Wild game thrives on the moors and mountains of Cumbria, and certain types of game have become associated with particular areas; for example, Derwentwater is associated with wild duck, Crossthwaite with pigeons, Underbarrow with pheasants and Greystoke with hares.

Derwent Water, Ashness Bridge 1893 32871

RECIPE

—·—

Duck with Cumberland Sauce

Cumberland Sauce is made with redcurrant jelly, port, orange and spices, and makes a delicious accompaniment to meat, poultry, game and sausages. It can be served either hot or cold.

> 4 duck portions
> Very thinly grated rind and juice of 1 lemon
> Very thinly grated rind and juice of 1 orange
> 4 tablespoonfuls of redcurrant jelly
> 4 tablespoonfuls of port
> A pinch of ground ginger
> A pinch of cayenne pepper
> 1 tablespoonful of brandy
> Salt and pepper

Pre-heat the oven to 190°C/375°/Gas Mark 5.

Place a rack in a roasting tin. Prick the duck portions all over with a fork, then sprinkle each portion with salt and pepper. Place the duck portions on the rack in the roasting tin and cook in the pre-heated oven for 45-50 minutes, until the duck skin is crisp and the juices run clear.

Meanwhile, make the Cumberland Sauce by blanching the lemon and orange rinds together in a small saucepan of boiling water for 5 minutes, then drain and keep the peel to one side. Melt the redcurrant jelly in another pan, then stir in the port, orange and lemon juice, ginger, cayenne pepper and salt to taste, and boil for 15 minutes. Add the blanched peel and heat through.

When the duck portions are cooked, transfer them to a serving dish and keep warm. Pour off the fat from the roasting dish, leaving the cooking juices. Place the roasting tin over a low heat and add the brandy, stirring well to dislodge the sediment in the roasting tin, then bring to the boil and stir in the Cumberland Sauce. Serve the duck portions with the sauce poured over.

—·—

Ulverston, King Street 1912 64396

Dialect Words from Cumbria

'Clarty' – dirty.

'Clegs' – horseflies and midges.

'Gammerstang' – an awkward person.

'Hoozer' – large.

'Jennyspinner' – a daddy-long-legs.

'Keks' – trousers.

'Kysty' – fussy or squeamish.

'Ladgefull' – embarrassing.

'Lug' – ear.

'Partles' – rabbit droppings.

'Twinters' – two-year-old sheep.

'Twitchbell' – an earwig.

'Urchins' – hedgehogs.

'Wuzzles' or **'wizzles'** – weasels.

'Dozzle' – a small amount of something.

'Scrow' – untidy.

'Slape' – slippery or smooth.

'Lakin' – playing.

The World Gurning Championship

One of England's most eccentric events takes place at the Cumbrian village of Egremont, near Whitehaven, every September – the World Gurning Championship. Gurning is the art of making grotesque faces, and the winner of this event is the person who receives the most applause from the audience for pulling a grotesque expression whilst looking through a horse's collar. The Gurning Championships take place during the Egremont Crab Apple Fair, which dates back to 1267 when it was first held to celebrate the local lord of the manor wheeling a cart of crab apples through the village to distribute to the poor. Crab apples are sour and bitter, and it may be that the gurning competition originated from the faces that the village people made as they bit into the sharp-tasting apples.

VEGETABLE DISHES

— . —

RECIPE

— . —

Pease Pudding

'Pease Pudding Hot!'

Pease Pudding has been a popular snack in the north of England for hundreds of years, and was commonly sold by street vendors in the 19th century. It can be eaten by itself, or as an accompaniment to roast pork, ham or bacon, or slices can be fried in bacon dripping to serve for breakfast.

> 225g/8oz yellow split peas
> 1 onion, finely chopped
> 25g/1oz butter
> 1 beaten egg
> Stock – bacon stock is best
> Salt and pepper

Soak the peas overnight, then drain. Put the peas and chopped onion in a pan, with enough stock to cover them. Bring to the boil, then cover the pan with the lid, reduce the heat and simmer until the peas are quite soft, adding more stock if necessary. Allow to cool slightly, then sieve or liquidise. Beat in the butter and egg, and test for seasoning.

Pour the mixture into a greased pie dish, cover with a lid or foil and cook for half an hour in a pre-heated oven at 160°C/325°F/Gas Mark 3.

— . —

Webb's Lettuce

Clarence Webb was a noted Kendal horticulturist who was very interested in producing improved varieties of flowers and vegetables. During the food shortages of the First World War he tried without success to promote allotments for people to grow their own food. One of his greatest successes was the development of a variety of lettuce known as 'Webb's Wonderful Lettuce', which is still popular today. Clarence Webb's shop in Kendal can be seen in this photograph, to the left of the Fleece Inn.

Kendal, Highgate, The Fleece Inn 1914 67372

RECITE

— · —

Leek and Bacon Pie

Leeks are popular vegetables in the north of England, and there are still places where contests are held to find the local leek-growing champion, such as that held by the Aspatria and District Leek Club at their annual show every September. This pie can be eaten hot or cold.

175g/6oz shortcrust pastry
450g/1 lb leeks, washed and trimmed
75g/3oz bacon rashers with the rinds
   removed
Freshly ground black pepper
300ml/ ½ pint chicken stock
1 bay leaf
1 egg
2 tablespoonfuls double cream

For glazing:
1 egg
Half a level teaspoonful salt

Pre-heat the oven to 150°C/300°F/Gas Mark 2.

Cut the washed and trimmed leeks diagonally into 1cm (half inch) slices and put them into an 18-20cm (7-8 inch) greased pie dish. Cut the bacon into small pieces and mix it with the leeks. Season well with freshly ground black pepper, add the bay leaf and pour in enough stock to just cover. Put the pie on the centre shelf of the pre-heated oven and cook for 1½ hours, or until the liquid has almost evaporated. Take out the pie from the oven and allow it to cool slightly, and remove the bay leaf.

Beat the egg and cream together and stir into the leek mixture. Roll out the pastry on a lightly floured surface to make a lid for the pie. Moisten the edge of the pie dish and cover the filling with the pastry. Trim the edges and crimp to seal, and make a small slit in the pastry lid to allow steam to escape whilst cooking. Beat the second egg and salt together and brush over the pastry to give it a glaze whilst cooking.

Increase the oven temperature to 200°C/400°F/Gas Mark 6. Cook the pie on the centre shelf of the hot oven for about 30 minutes, or until the pastry is crisp and golden brown. Leave the pie to cool slightly before serving if eating hot.

— · —

RECIPE

—·—

Cumberland Herb Pudding

This recipe includes the optional ingredient of nettles. The young shoots of nettles have been eaten in the spring by country people for centuries, as a welcome source of fresh greens at the time of year known as the 'hungry gap' before other vegetables are ready to eat. Only the tender top sprigs of nettles should be eaten, and can be cooked in the same way as spinach, or made into a tasty soup with pieces of bacon and milk. The acid which causes the nettles to sting is destroyed by cooking.

1 heaped tablespoonful of pearl barley
450g/1 lb spring cabbage, washed and shredded
115g/4oz nettles, washed (optional, but worth trying!)
2 onions, peeled and finely chopped
2 leeks, washed, trimmed and finely chopped
25g/1oz butter
1 egg
Salt and pepper

Soak the pearl barley overnight in 1 pint of water. The next day, boil it in the same water until it is tender. Place the prepared vegetables (including the nettles, if used) in a large, heavy saucepan and add the cooked barley and the water in which it was cooked. Add a little more water if necessary, so that all the ingredients are covered. Bring to the boil and continue boiling quickly until all the vegetables are tender, keeping the lid on the pan, stirring occasionally to make sure that no barley sticks to the base of the pan – this can take between 20-30 minutes, depending on the age and quality of the vegetables. When cooked, drain through a colander, discarding the liquid, and put the vegetables and barley back into the pan. Add the butter and beaten egg, season to taste with salt and pepper, and mix it all together well.

Pre-heat the oven to 180°C/350°F/Gas Mark 4.

Turn the mixture into a greased 1.2 litre (2 pint) ovenproof dish. Cover with foil and place in the pre-heated oven for 15 minutes. Serve hot, turned out of the basin onto a warmed serving dish.

—·—

Sedbergh, Market Place 1894 34077

RECIPE

~ · ~

Hot Red Cabbage

This is a traditional accompaniment to rich meat, such as venison, game, pork and ham.

1 red cabbage
2 cooking apples
1 tablespoonful soft brown sugar
1 onion
600ml/1 pint water
4 tablespoonfuls of red wine
A few cloves (optional)
Salt and pepper

Shred the cabbage, and discard the core. Peel, core and slice the apples, and peel and chop the onion. Place the cabbage, apple and onion in a large saucepan with the sugar, salt, pepper, red wine, water and cloves (if using). Bring to the boil, then reduce heat, cover the pan and simmer gently for 2 hours. Strain when cooked, and serve hot as an accompaniment to meat.

~ · ~

Kirkby Lonsdale, Market Square 1908 59539

PUDDINGS AND DESSERTS

Grasmere, Dove Cottage 1936 87636

Dorothy Wordsworth, sister of the poet William Wordsworth, lived with her brother between 1799 and 1808 in Dove Cottage at Grasmere. She kept a diary, and occasionally noted a meal or a cooking session. Her diary entry for 16 May 1800 mentioned a dish called Hasty Pudding:

"…I finished my letter to M.H. Ate hasty pudding and went to bed."

RECIPE

⁓ · ⁓

Hasty Pudding

There are many versions of Hasty Pudding, but the essence of it is that it is indeed hastily made, using oatmeal. It is then sweetened with sugar, and perhaps flavoured with cinnamon or nutmeg, and ends up rather like porridge. Other ingredients might be added, depending on what was to hand.

> 600ml/1 pint milk
> 225g/8oz oatmeal
> 1 egg yolk
> A pinch of salt
> 50g/2oz soft brown sugar
> A pinch of ground cinnamon or freshly grated nutmeg
> Cream to serve

Mix the oatmeal, salt, egg yolk and sugar together with a little of the milk. Heat the remaining milk, and just before it boils, add the oatmeal mixture. Boil for a few minutes, stirring all the time, until the mixture thickens, then reduce the heat and simmer for a few minutes. Serve hot, sprinkled with cinnamon or nutmeg, and cream, or a spoonful of jam if preferred.

⁓ · ⁓

RECIPE

~—∙—~

Damson and Apple Tansy

Cumbria is famous for its damsons, especially those grown in the Lyth valley, just south of Windermere. These damsons are known locally as Witherslack damsons, after the village of that name, and are large, juicy and much sweeter than damsons grown elsewhere in the country. They are often eaten raw, like grapes, and accompanied by a piece of Lancashire cheese.

This old English recipe dates back to the 15th century, and took its name from the bitter-tasting herb of tansy which was used in the past for flavouring sweet dishes – however, 'tansy' is now used to describe a buttered fruit purée made with eggs and breadcrumbs, and the flavour is sharpened with lemon juice instead.

> 225/8oz damsons
> 225g/8oz cooking apples
> 50g/2oz unsalted butter
> 115g/4oz caster sugar
> 2 egg yolks, beaten
> 4 level dessertspoonfuls of fresh white breadcrumbs
> 150ml/ ¼ pint double cream
> 1 dessertspoonful of lemon juice

Wash the damsons. Peel and core the apples and cut them into thin slices. Melt the butter in a heavy-bottomed saucepan with 70ml (2½ fl oz) of cold water, cover the pan with its lid and boil the fruit over a low heat until it is soft, stirring from time to time to prevent sticking and burning. Remove the pan from the heat and either push the fruit though a coarse sieve or put it through a blender, to form a purée. Return the purée to the pan and stir in the sugar – add a little extra to taste if necessary. If the purée seems rather thin, cook it over a low heat until it has reduced down and thickened to a dropping consistency. Remove the pan from the heat and allow the purée to cool a little, then mix in the beaten egg and the breadcrumbs. Return the pan to a low heat and cook, stirring continually, until the mixture has thickened, then leave to cool.

Lightly whisk the cream and fold it into the cooled damson mixture. Add a little lemon juice to taste, to sharpen the flavour. Spoon the mixture into individual serving dishes or glasses and chill in the refrigerator for at least one hour before serving.

~—∙—~

Newby Bridge 1914 67414a

RECIPE

— · —

Damson Fool

900g/2 lbs damsons
225g/8oz caster sugar
600ml/1 pint milk
300ml/ ½ pint double cream
4 egg yolks
1 tablespoonful lemon juice
A little extra double cream for decoration

Stew the damsons with the sugar and a very small amount of water in a saucepan gently over a very low heat until they are soft and tender. Put the fruit through a sieve to remove the skins and stones, then allow the fruit purée to cool.

Mix the milk and cream together and heat in a saucepan to boiling point. Whisk the egg yolks in a separate bowl, then pour a little of the boiling milk mixture onto the egg yolks and continue whisking. Pour the egg mixture into the saucepan with the milk, and cook over a low heat until the mixture thickens to form a custard, stirring continually. When the mixture has thickened, remove from the heat and allow to cool. Mix the damson purée with the custard and stir in the lemon juice. Pour the mixture either into one large serving dish or individual glass dishes. Keep in the fridge until ready to serve, decorated with a little whipped cream.

— · —

Penrith, The Clock Tower 1893
32923v

Bowness-on-Windermere, The Ferry Boat 1896 38800

RECIPE

—.—

Coniston Pudding

For the pastry:
175g/6oz plain flour
75g/3oz butter or margarine
25g/1oz caster sugar
1 egg

For the filling:
25g/1oz caster sugar
1 egg
A pinch of freshly grated nutmeg
150ml/ ¼ pint (total) hot milk
   mixed with single cream
25g/1oz raisins
25g/1oz currants
15g/ ½ oz chopped candied peel

Rub the butter into the flour until the mixture resembles fine breadcrumbs, then add the sugar and mix well. Beat in the egg, and mix it well in to form a soft dough. Leave it to rest for 30 minutes, then roll out the dough on a lightly floured surface and use it to line a greased 20cm (8 inch) flan or pie dish.

Pre-heat the oven to 180°C/350°F/Gas Mark 4 and place a baking sheet in the hot oven to heat up whilst you prepare the filling.

Make the filling by beating the egg and adding the sugar and freshly grated nutmeg. Add the hot milk and cream mixture, the raisins, currants and candied peel, and mix well. Pour the mixture into the pastry case, place the flan or pie dish on the pre-heated baking tray (this will help the pastry at the base of the pudding to cook through) and bake in the oven for about 50 minutes.

—.—

Coniston, The Village 1929 82798

RECITE

—·—

Gooseberry Pie

Not much soft fruit is grown in this cold area of the country, but damsons and gooseberries are notable exceptions. In many parts of England a gooseberry pudding or pie was the traditional fare for Whit Sunday (50 days after Easter). This is the day on which the Christian Church celebrates Pentecost, the time when the Holy Spirit descended on the Apostles.

> 225g/8oz shortcrust pastry
> 450g/1 lb gooseberries
> 115g/4oz caster sugar
> 1 teaspoonful of lemon juice
> 1 egg yolk
> A little milk, to glaze

Pre-heat the oven to 230°C/450°F/Gas Mark 8.

Top and tail the gooseberries and put them into a saucepan with the sugar and a little water. Simmer gently until soft. Mash the fruit to a pulp and add the lemon juice. Leave the fruit pulp to cool, then stir in the egg yolk.

Grease a 20cm (8 inch) pie dish or sandwich tin. Roll out two-thirds of the pastry on a lightly-floured surface, and use it to line the pie dish or tin. Put the fruit pulp into the dish. Roll out the remaining pastry and use it to make a lid for the pie, trim, and crimp the edges to seal. Make two slits in the pastry case to allow steam to escape during cooking. Brush the top of the pie with a little milk to glaze, then bake in the pre-heated oven for 30-40 minutes, until the pastry is golden brown. Serve with cream or custard, and extra sugar to taste, if necessary.

—·—

RECIPE

Westmorland Three Deckers

350g/12oz flour
A pinch of salt
175g/6oz butter or margarine
A little cold water
450g/1 lb plums or large damsons, cut in half and their
　　stones removed
50g/2oz caster sugar
A little milk to glaze

Sift the flour and salt into a bowl, then rub in the butter or margarine until the mixture resembles fine breadcrumbs. Add enough cold water to mix it all into a soft dough, knead lightly and leave to rest in a cool place for 30 minutes.

Pre-heat the oven to 190°C/375°F/Gas Mark 5.

Divide the dough into three equal pieces. Roll out one piece on a lightly-floured surface and use it to line a greased pie plate or tin. Place half the plums or damsons in the pie dish and sprinkle half the sugar over them. Roll out the second piece of dough and place it over the fruit. Put the remaining plums or damsons on top, and sprinkle with the remaining sugar. Roll out the last piece of dough and place it on top. Brush the top with a little milk to glaze, then bake in the pre-heated oven for about 1 hour, until the pastry is crisp and golden. Serve with cream or custard, and a little extra sugar if needed.

Ulverston, Market Place 1912 64395

RECIPE

— . —

Cumberland Apple Pudding

75g/3oz self-raising flour
75g/3oz fresh breadcrumbs
75g/3oz shredded suet
75g/3oz soft brown sugar
2 large eggs, beaten
1 large cooking apple
Grated rind of 1 lemon
A pinch of freshly grated nutmeg
1 tablespoonful golden syrup, warmed
4-6 tablespoonfuls milk
A pinch of salt

Grease a 1.2 litre (2 pint) pudding basin.

Mix together the flour, breadcrumbs, suet, sugar, lemon rind and salt.
Peel, core and finely chop the apple, then stir the apple into the flour
mixture together with the warmed syrup and the beaten eggs, adding
just enough milk to form a soft dough, and mix it all thoroughly. Place
the mixture into the greased pudding basin.

Cover the top of the basin with pleated greaseproof paper (to allow
room for rising), and then a piece of foil and tie down firmly with string.
Place the basin in a large saucepan of boiling water, cover the pan with
its lid, and steam for about 1½ hours. Top up the pan with more boiling
water from time to time, and be sure not to let the pan boil dry.

When cooked, turn out the pudding onto a serving dish and serve
piping hot, with custard or cream.

— . —

Sedbergh, Haymaking 1924 75815x

RECIPE

Sticky Toffee Pudding

The pretty village of Cartmel in southern Cumbria is the home of The Sticky Toffee Pudding Company. Sticky Toffee Pudding is one of Britain's great puddings, and the sort of dish which prompted a 17th-century Frenchman to write: 'Ah, what an excellent thing is an English pudding! To come in pudding time is, as much to say, to come in the most lucky moment in the world!'.

For the pudding:
225g/8oz whole Medjool dates
1 teaspoonful vanilla extract
175g/6oz self-raising flour, plus a little extra for
   preparing the pudding tins
1 teaspoonful bicarbonate of soda
2 eggs, beaten
75g/3oz butter, softened, plus extra for greasing
150g/5oz demerara sugar
2 tablespoonfuls black treacle, warmed
150ml/ ¼ pint milk

For the toffee sauce:
175g/6oz light muscovado sugar
50g/2oz butter, cut into small pieces
300ml/ ½ pint double cream
1 tablespoonful black treacle

Stone the dates and chop them into quite small pieces, put them in a bowl, then pour just enough boiling water over to cover them. Leave for about 30 minutes until they are cool and well-soaked, then mash the soaked dates roughly with a fork. Stir in the vanilla extract. Butter the insides of seven mini pudding tins (each about 200ml/7fl oz) and sprinkle lightly with a little flour, and place them on a baking sheet.

Pre-heat the oven to 180C°/350°F/Gas Mark 4.

While the dates are soaking, make the puddings. Mix the flour and bicarbonate of soda together. Beat the eggs in a separate bowl. Beat the butter and sugar together in a large bowl for a few minutes until the mixture is fluffy and creamy. Gradually add the beaten eggs, a little at a time, beating the mixture well between additions. Beat in the warmed black treacle. Using a large metal spoon, gently fold in one-third of the flour, then half the milk, being careful not to over-beat the mixture. Repeat until all the flour and milk has been used. Stir the soaked and mashed dates into the pudding batter, which will be soft and thick. Spoon the mixture evenly between the individual pudding tins, place them on a baking tray or in a roasting dish and bake in the pre-heated oven for 20-25 minutes, until they are risen and firm.

Whilst the puddings are cooking, make the sauce: put the sugar and butter for the sauce into a medium saucepan with half the cream. Bring to the boil over a medium heat, stirring all the time, until the sugar has completely dissolved. Stir in the black treacle, turn up the heat slightly and let the mixture bubble away for 2-3 minutes until it is a rich toffee colour, stirring occasionally to ensure the sauce doesn't burn. Take the pan off the heat, allow to cool for a few minutes and beat in the rest of the cream.

Remove the puddings from the oven. Leave them in their tins for a few minutes, then loosen them well from the sides of the tins with a small palette knife before turning them out. Serve the puddings hot, with the sauce drizzled over, accompanied by cream or custard.

To make the puddings even stickier, you can pour the sauce over them and then leave them to stand for a day or two, coated in the sauce. To do this, pour about half the sauce into one or two ovenproof serving dishes. Sit the turned-out puddings on the sauce, and then pour the rest of the sauce over them. Cover the dishes loosely with foil, and leave the puddings to stand in a cool place until needed, when they can be re-heated in the oven (180C°/350°F/Gas Mark 4), still covered in foil, until the sauce is bubbling.

Cartmel, Ducks on the Beck 1914 67410x

TEATIME AND BAKING

In former centuries the port of Whitehaven traded with the West Indies, exchanging locally-produced wool for ginger, rum, treacle, exotic fruit, brown sugar and spices, all of which figure prominently in traditional fare from Cumbria, such as Cumberland Rum Nickie, Ginger Scones and Lemon Cake.

RECITE

~·~

Cumbrian Lemon Cake

115g/4oz butter, softened to room temperature
50g/2oz lard
150g/5oz caster sugar
2 eggs, beaten
225g/8oz self-raising flour
2 tablespoonfuls lemon juice
Finely-grated rind of 1 lemon
50g/2oz candied lemon peel, finely chopped
1 tablespoonful milk
Icing sugar, to finish

Pre-heat the oven to 180°C/350°F/Gas Mark 4.

Grease an 18-20cm (7-8 inch) cake tin with a removable base. Cream the butter, lard and sugar together until light and fluffy. Gradually mix in the beaten eggs, a little at a time, adding 1 tablespoonful of the flour at the same time to prevent the mixture curdling. Mix thoroughly, then fold in the rest of the flour with a large metal spoon.

Add the lemon juice, the finely grated lemon rind and the chopped candied lemon peel. Mix well, and only add the tablespoonful of milk if the mixture seems too stiff – you should end up with a firm, dropping consistency.

Pour the mixture into the prepared cake tin and bake in the centre of the pre-heated oven for about 1 hour. Check that the cake is cooked by inserting a small metal skewer into the centre, which will come out clean when the cake is ready. If necessary, continue cooking for up to a further 30 minutes.

Leave to cool in the tin before removing and leaving to cool completely on a wire rack. Sift icing sugar across the top before serving. This can also be made into a lemon sandwich-style cake if you cut it across into two rounds, spread one side with lemon curd, and then sandwich the two rounds back together.

~·~

RECITE

— . —

Cumberland Rum Nickies

For the pastry:
225g/8oz plain flour
115g/4oz butter or margarine
A pinch of salt
A little cold water
A little milk to glaze

For the filling:
115g/4oz currants
25g/1oz brown sugar
Half a teaspoonful grated nutmeg
25g/1oz butter or margarine
1 tablespoonful rum

To make the filling mixture: melt the butter in a large saucepan, and add the rum and nutmeg. Add the sugar and currants and leave to steep for about 1 hour.

To make the pastry: sift the flour and salt together into a bowl and then rub in the butter or margarine until the mixture resembles fine breadcrumbs. Add enough cold water to mix to a soft dough. Knead lightly until the dough is smooth and elastic, then leave to rest in a cool place for 30 minutes.

Pre-heat the oven to 200°C/400°F/Gas Mark 6.

Roll out the pastry on a lightly-floured surface and cut it into rounds about 8cm (3 inches) in diameter. Place a spoonful of the filling mixture on to half the pastry circles. Cover each filled circle with the remaining pastry circles, moistening the edges and pinching well to seal. Prick the top of each Nickie with a fork to make holes to allow steam to escape whilst cooking, and brush with milk to glaze. Place the Nickies on a greased baking sheet and bake in the pre-heated oven for about 12-15 minutes, until the pastry is crisp and golden brown.

— . —

Hawkshead, The Village 1896 38831

RECIPE

— · —

Gingerbread

Gingerbread is popular all over Britain, but the Cumbrian village of Grasmere is especially famous for it. There are actually two varieties of gingerbread linked with Grasmere, one being thin and the other twice as thick. The thicker version is probably the original 'local' version, which was originally made and given as payment for people doing work for the church. The thinner version is believed to have been introduced by Sarah Nelson who came to the village from Lancashire and set up business there in the 1850s, and it is her version for which the village is now famous. Sarah Nelson's gingerbread recipe has been kept a closely-guarded secret, but this recipe is similar.

225g/8oz oatmeal
2 teaspoonfuls ground ginger
Half a teaspoonful bicarbonate of soda
Half a teaspoonful cream of tartar
1 tablespoonful golden syrup
175g/6oz soft brown sugar
115g/4oz butter or margarine

Pre-heat the oven to 160°C/325°F/Gas Mark 3.

Mix together the oatmeal, ginger, bicarbonate of soda and cream of tartar. Melt the syrup, butter or margarine and sugar together in a saucepan over a gentle heat, then add to the dry ingredients, mixing it well together. Press the mixture into a well-greased 20cm (8inch) shallow tin, and bake in the pre-heated oven for about 45 minutes. When cooked, remove from the oven and mark the gingerbread into squares, but leave it to cool in the tin before taking it out.

— · —

Grasmere, Red Lion Square 1926 79206

Grasmere's Rushbearing Festival

Grasmere's church is dedicated to St Oswald, whose feast day is 5th August. This is celebrated in Grasmere on the nearest Saturday to 5th August with a Rushbearing Festival, commemorating a custom that dates back to the days when the earthen floors of

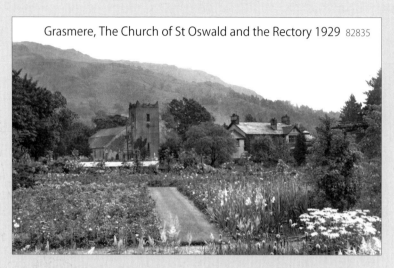

Grasmere, The Church of St Oswald and the Rectory 1929 82835

churches were strewn with rushes or straw to make the floor softer underfoot; this covering was renewed before major festivals and, as at Grasmere, before the church's dedication day. At Grasmere, children parade through the village carrying rushes and decorations for the church. After the procession and a special service in the church, the children who have carried the rushes are traditionally given a piece of Grasmere Gingerbread.

The church at Grasmere is also famous for its graveyard being the resting-place of William Wordsworth, his wife Mary and their children Dora, William, Thomas and Catherine, and Wordsworth's sister Dorothy.

Grasmere, The Churchyard, Wordsworth's Grave c1880 G45501

Buttermere, Haymaking c1955 B260064

RECIPE

—.—

Kendal Wigs

There are several recipes for these small buns from Cumbria, known variously as Wigs, Wiggs or Whigs. Hawkshead also has its own version, which is flavoured with caraway seeds.

> 450g/1 lb plain flour
> 50g/2oz lard
> 50g/2oz soft brown sugar
> 25g/1oz fresh yeast, or 3 teaspoonfuls quick-acting dried yeast
> 300ml/½ pint warm water
> A pinch of salt
> 25g/1oz currants

Dissolve the sugar in the warm water, add the yeast, then leave it for about ten minutes, until it becomes frothy. Rub the lard into the flour and add a pinch of salt. When the yeast mixture is ready, pour it into the dry ingredients and mix it all to form a soft dough, adding a little milk if necessary. Knead the dough for about ten minutes, until it is smooth and elastic, then knead the currants into the dough.

Leave the dough to rise in a warm place, in a bowl covered with a clean cloth or inside a greased polythene bag, until it has doubled in size. Divide the dough into about 20 small pieces and shape them into buns. Place the buns on greased baking sheets, well spaced out, and leave to rise again in a warm place for about 1 hour, then bake in a pre-heated oven for about 15 minutes (200°C/400°F/Gas Mark 6). Serve warm.

—.—

Kendal, Stricklandgate 1888 21088

RECITE

— . —

Westmorland Pepper Cake

An unusual recipe from the area is Westmorland Pepper Cake, which was traditionally made at Christmas time and offered to carol singers as they came around. Although this cake does contain pepper, its name probably also refers to the use of ground allspice in the recipe, which was also called clove pepper in the north of England.

75g/3oz raisins
75g/3oz currants
115g/4oz caster sugar
75g/3oz butter or margarine
225g/8oz self-raising flour
A pinch of salt
Half a teaspoonful ground ginger
A large pinch of ground allspice (ground cloves)
Half a teaspoonful finely ground black pepper
4 tablespoonfuls milk
1 egg, beaten

Pre-heat the oven to 180°C/350°F/Gas Mark 4.

Grease the base of a deep 18-20cm (7-8 inch) round cake tin and line the base with greaseproof paper. Put the dried fruit, sugar, butter or margarine and 150ml (¼ pint) of water into a saucepan and bring to the boil. Simmer for 10 minutes, then remove the pan from the heat and leave to cool for a few minutes. Put the flour, salt, spices and pepper into a large bowl and gently stir in the fruit mixture, milk and the beaten egg. Mix thoroughly together, but without beating.

Turn the mixture into the prepared cake tin and bake in the pre-heated oven for about 50 minutes, or until the top of the cake is firm to the touch and golden brown. Turn out and leave to cool on a wire rack.

— . —

Nut Monday

In the Kendal area, whole families once went out into the woods and hedgerows on the public holiday in September to forage for nuts to augment their winter food supplies. The day was known as Nut Monday. This custom fell out of favour by the 1860s and the holiday was abolished.

Kendal, Children 1914 67387x

RECIPE

— . —

Windermere Spice Biscuits

225g/8oz butter or margarine

225g/8oz soft brown sugar

350g/12oz self-raising flour

1-2 teaspoonfuls caraway seeds

1 teaspoonful ground cinnamon

2 eggs, beaten

Pre-heat the oven to 180°C/350°F/Gas Mark 4.

Cream together the butter or margarine and sugar. Add the flour, caraway seeds and cinnamon, and gradually beat in the eggs to the mixture to form a dough. Knead the dough to mix all the ingredients well together, until it is soft and smooth. Roll out the dough on a lightly-floured surface to about 1cm (half an inch) thick. Cut into small biscuit rounds with a cutter, and place the rounds on a greased baking sheet. Bake in the pre-heated oven for 20-30 minutes until the biscuits are golden but not browned, then cool on a wire rack.

— . —

Langdale Pikes, The Valley 1892 30518

Coniston, Waterhead
1912 64281

MISCELLANEOUS

Ambleside, Bridge House 1912 64306

RECIPE

—·—

Cumberland Rum Butter

Cumberland rum butter is a delicious regional speciality of butter flavoured with rum, Barbados sugar and spices. It was traditionally made to celebrate the birth of a baby, and was served with oatcakes (see recipe on page 84) to well-wishers who came to visit the new arrival. The mother-to-be would make the rum butter before her baby was due, and keep it in a traditional rum butter bowl. It was the custom in some parts of Cumbria for the visitors to place coins in the empty butter bowl when all the rum butter had been consumed, to ensure that the newborn child would have a long and prosperous life. Nowadays, rum butter is delicious eaten with scones or steamed puddings, and especially with mince pies and Christmas pudding.

> 225g/8oz unsalted butter, softened to room temperature
> 350g/12oz soft brown sugar
> 125ml/4 fl oz dark rum
> A good pinch of ground cinnamon
> A good pinch of ground nutmeg

Beat the butter in a bowl until it is soft and creamy. Beat in the sugar until it is thoroughly blended. Gradually add the rum, beating well after each addition. Add cinnamon and nutmeg to taste, and put the mixture into a small pot or jar. Cover and store in the refrigerator, and chill well before serving. This will keep well in the refrigerator for several weeks.

—·—

RECIPE

—·—

Oatcakes

Oatcakes were once a staple food in the north of England. They are delicious eaten with cheese, or spread with jam, marmalade or Cumberland rum butter – see page 83.

> 115g/4oz plain flour
> 115g/4oz rolled oats
> 25g/1oz caster sugar
> 50g/2oz butter or margarine
> 25g/1oz lard
> A pinch of salt
> Half a teaspoonful bicarbonate of soda
> 1 tablespoonful water
> A little milk

Pre-heat the oven to 190°C/375°F/Gas Mark 5.

Sieve the flour into a bowl, and add the rolled oats, sugar and salt. Melt the butter or margarine and lard with the bicarbonate of soda and water in a saucepan, then add to the dry ingredients and mix well, adding just enough milk to form the mixture into a firm dough.

Roll out the dough on a lightly floured surface to about 5mm (¼ inch) thick. Cut out into small circles with a biscuit cutter. Place on a greased baking sheet, well spaced out, and bake in the pre-heated oven for about 15 minutes, until the oatcakes are golden brown.

—·—

Kendal Mint Cake

It is said that Joseph Wiper was the first person to make Kendal Mint Cake, although others claim that honour. It is a combination of sugar, glucose and peppermint and is a favourite with walkers, athletes and mountaineers as it gives energy quickly. Sir Edmund Hillary and Sirdar Tensing took it to the summit of Everest when they made their historic first ascent of the world's highest mountain in 1953.

Helvellyn, Striding Edge 1912 64344

INDEX OF PHOTOGRAPHS

⁓ ∙ ⁓

⁓ ∙ ⁓

INDEX OF RECIPES

NOTES

FREE PRINT OF YOUR CHOICE

Mounted Print
Overall size 14 x 11 inches (355 x 280mm)

Choose any Frith photograph in this book.
Simply complete the Voucher opposite and return it with your remittance for £3.50 (to cover postage and handling) and we will print the photograph of your choice in SEPIA (size 11 x 8 inches) and supply it in a cream mount with a burgundy rule line (overall size 14 x 11 inches).
Please note: aerial photographs and photographs with a reference number starting with a "Z" are not Frith photographs and cannot be supplied under this offer. Offer valid for delivery to one UK address only.

PLUS: Order additional Mounted Prints at HALF PRICE - £9.50 each (normally £19.00)
If you would like to order more Frith prints from this book, possibly as gifts for friends and family, you can buy them at half price (with no additional postage and handling costs).

PLUS: Have your Mounted Prints framed
For an extra £18.00 per print you can have your mounted print(s) framed in an elegant polished wood and gilt moulding, overall size 16 x 13 inches (no additional postage and handling required).

IMPORTANT!

These special prices are only available if you use this form to order. You must use the ORIGINAL VOUCHER on this page (no copies permitted). We can only despatch to one UK address. This offer cannot be combined with any other offer.

Send completed Voucher form to:
The Francis Frith Collection, Frith's Barn, Teffont, Salisbury, Wiltshire SP3 5QP

CHOOSE A PHOTOGRAPH FROM THIS BOOK

Voucher for **FREE** *and Reduced Price Frith Prints*

Please do not photocopy this voucher. Only the original is valid, so please fill it in, cut it out and return it to us with your order.

Picture ref no	Page no	Qty	Mounted @ £9.50	Framed + £18.00	Total Cost £
		1	Free of charge*	£	£
			£9.50	£	£
			£9.50	£	£
			£9.50	£	£
			£9.50	£	£
			£9.50	£	£
			* Post & handling		£3.50
			Total Order Cost		£

Please allow 28 days for delivery. Offer available to one UK address only

Title of this book . . . .

I enclose a cheque/postal order for £ . . . .

made payable to 'The Francis Frith Collection'

OR please debit my Mastercard / Visa / Maestro card, details below

Card Number

Issue No (Maestro only)   Valid from (Maestro)

Expires   Signature

Name Mr/Mrs/Ms . . . .

Address . . . .

. . . .

. . . .

. . . . Postcode . . . .

Daytime Tel No . . . .

Email . . . .

978-1-84589-438-2   Valid to 31/12/11

Can you help us with information about any of the Frith photographs in this book?

We are gradually compiling an historical record for each of the photographs in the Frith archive. It is always fascinating to find out the names of the people shown in the pictures, as well as insights into the shops, buildings and other features depicted.

If you recognize anyone in the photographs in this book, or if you have information not already included in the author's caption, do let us know. We would love to hear from you, and will try to publish it in future books or articles.

An Invitation from The Francis Frith Collection to Share Your Memories

The 'Share Your Memories' feature of our website allows members of the public to add personal memories relating to the places featured in our photographs, or comment on others already added. Seeing a place from your past can rekindle forgotten or long held memories. Why not visit the website, find photographs of places you know well and add YOUR story for others to read and enjoy? We would love to hear from you!

www.francisfrith.com/memories

Our production team

Frith books are produced by a small dedicated team at offices in the converted Grade II listed 18th-century barn at Teffont near Salisbury, illustrated above. Most have worked with the Frith Collection for many years. All have in common one quality: they have a passion for the Frith Collection.

Frith Books and Gifts

We have a wide range of books and gifts available on our website utilising our photographic archive, many of which can be individually personalised.

www.francisfrith.com